Grandpa

I want to hear your story

The Life Graduate Publishing Group

We love to receive reviews from our customers. If you had the opportunity to provide a review we would greatly appreciate it.

Thank you!

A Place to Share My Life Memories.

Grandpa xx

My Lifetime Legacy

Journal

THE BEGINNING...

Baby Grandpa

Grandpa's Introduction

Before I start....just a brief introduction about me!

_____

_____

_____

_____

_____

_____

_____

_____

_____

_____

Name:

Signature:

Date:

THE BEGINNING.....

Full Name at Birth

_____

Date of Birth   /   /_____

Time of Birth   :_____

Day of the week you were born?_____

Height at birth? (if known)_____

Weight at birth? (If known)_____

Your Place of Birth (include the City/Town, Country)

_____

Did you have any siblings when you were born? If so, what were their names and their ages?

_____

_____

_____

ADD ANY ADDITIONAL NOTES OR INFORMATION HERE...

THE BEGINNING.....

Share with us some information about your parents?

_____

_____

_____

_____

_____

Were you in good health as a baby?

_____

_____

_____

Did you have any unique characteristics or funny things you did as a baby?

_____

_____

_____

_____

IF YOU HAVE ANY EARLY BABY PHOTOS, INCLUDE THEM HERE...

THE BEGINNING.....

Were you an active or quiet baby?

_____

_____

_____

_____

_____

Were you ever told what your first words were?

_____

_____

How old were you when you first walked?

_____

_____

_____

_____

_____

THE
BEGINNING.....

Can you remember what you loved to play as a toddler?

_____

_____

_____

_____

_____

What is one of your earliest memories as a toddler?

_____

_____

_____

_____

_____

_____

_____

_____

THE
BEGINNING......

Did you attend pre-school or something similar when you were a toddler?

_____

_____

_____

_____

Do you have a photo when you were a toddler that you could include here?

THE BEGINNING. CONT...

Do you have any other memories or stories to share when you were a baby or a young child?

_____

_____

_____

_____

_____

_____

_____

_____

_____

_____

_____

_____

_____

"Every father should remember one day his son or daughter will follow his example, not his advice."
—Charles Kettering

FAMILY HISTORY

This is our Family Tree!

FAMILY HISTORY

My grandparents names were:

Grandmother (Fathers Side): _____

Grandfather (Fathers Side) _____

Grandmother (Mothers Side): _____

Grandfather (Mothers Side) _____

They were born in: (country)

Grandmother (Fathers Side): _____

Grandfather (Fathers Side) _____

Grandmother (Mothers Side): _____

Grandfather (Mothers Side) _____

This is something that not many people may know about our family history......

_____

_____

_____

_____

_____

_____

Our FAMILY
TREE

GrandFather
[ ]

GrandFather
[ ]

Grandmother
[ ]

Grandmother
[ ]

Mother
[ ]

Father
[ ]

Me
[ ]

ADD ANY ADDITIONAL NOTES OR INFORMATION HERE ABOUT YOUR FAMILY HISTORY..

_____

_____

_____

_____

_____

_____

_____

_____

_____

_____

_____

_____

_____

_____

_____

_____

CHILDHOOD YEARS

CHILDHOOD YEARS....

What was your favorite toy growing up?

_____

_____

_____

_____

Did you have a pet or any pets growing up?

_____

_____

_____

_____

What was your favorite T.V show to watch as a child?

_____

_____

_____

_____

Was there a moment you remember getting into big trouble as a child? Was there a punishment?

_____

_____

_____

_____

_____

Do you remember attending a special celebration or event that was very special to you?

_____

_____

_____

_____

_____

_____

_____

ADD ANY ADDITIONAL NOTES OR INFORMATION HERE...

CHILDHOOD YEARS....

What are your fondest memories growing up between the ages of 5 - 12 years?

_____

_____

_____

_____

_____

_____

_____

_____

_____

_____

_____

_____

_____

_____

IF YOU HAVE ANY EARLY CHILDHOOD PHOTOS, PLACE THEM HERE...

CHILDHOOD YEARS....

What was your favorite meal as a child?

_____

What elementary/primary school did you attend and where was it located?

_____

_____

Describe your most memorable moment or story from elementary/primary school.

_____

_____

_____

_____

_____

_____

_____

_____

CHILDHOOD YEARS....

Where did you grow up as a child?
(house, location, town etc)

_____

_____

_____

_____

Who was your best friend or your best friends as a child?

_____

_____

What was your favorite day of the week and why?

_____

_____

_____

_____

_____

_____

DO YOU HAVE ANY OTHER DETAILS TO SHARE?

_____

_____

_____

_____

_____

_____

_____

_____

_____

_____

_____

_____

_____

_____

DO YOU HAVE ANY SCHOOL PHOTOS YOU CAN INCLUDE HERE?

TEENAGE YEARS

TEENAGE YEARS....

Describe your dress sense and clothing as a teenager. Is there anything that stands out for you?

_____

_____

_____

_____

Who taught you how to drive?

_____

_____

_____

When and where did you learn to drive a vehicle?

_____

_____

_____

_____

TEENAGE YEARS.....

What was your first vehicle and how much did you purchase it for? Tell us your special 'first car' story!

_____

_____

_____

_____

_____

_____

_____

_____

_____

_____

_____

_____

_____

_____

INCLUE ANY 'FIRST VEHICLE' PHOTOS
OR OTHER INFORMATION HERE..

TEENAGE YEARS....

What High School did you attend and where was it located?

_____

_____

_____

_____

_____

Who was you favorite teacher or coach and why?

_____

_____

_____

_____

_____

_____

_____

What was your favorite subject at school?

_____

_____

_____

_____

_____

_____

_____

_____

Did you date anyone at High School? If so, tell us a story about it.

_____

_____

_____

_____

_____

_____

SHARE ANY FURTHER DETAILS HERE

TEENAGE YEARS....

What hobbies did you have as a teenager?

_____

_____

_____

What is your most memorable moment as a teenager?

_____

_____

_____

_____

_____

If you knew what you know today, what would you have done differently as a teenager?

_____

_____

_____

_____

_____

_____

SHARE ANY HIGH SCHOOL PHOTOS OR OTHER MEMORIES TO SHARE?

TEENAGE YEARS....

Did you have a close friendship group? Have you maintained contact with any of them?

_____

_____

_____

_____

_____

Did you have any nicknames at High School?

_____

_____

What 5 words come to mind to describe your teenage years?

1. _____

2. _____

3. _____

4. _____

5. _____

WHEN I WAS..

WHEN I WAS....

When I was a child, my mode of transport to school was..

_____

_____

When I was in my teens, the biggest news story that I recall was .....

_____

_____

_____

When I was growing up, my 3 favorite movies were:

1. _____

2. _____

3. _____

WHEN I WAS....

When I was a child, the first movie I went to the theatre to see was..

_____

When I graduated from elementary/primary school, the year was.. _____

When I was a child, I wanted to be a......

_____

When I was 18 years old, my favorite music and band was..

_____

When I was in my teens, the most popular thing to do on a Saturday night was.......

_____

_____

When I was young, I loved to travel to.......

_____

_____

_____

WHEN I WAS....

When I graduated from school, I celebrated by...

_____

_____

_____

_____

_____

_____

When I was a teenager, the one thing I wish I had attempted to do was....

_____

_____

_____

_____

_____

_____

_____

USE THE NEXT 2 PAGES TO SHARE SOME TRAVEL PHOTOS

PARENTHOOD

PARENTHOOD....

How old were you when you first became a parent?

_____

Explain how you felt emotionally when you became a father?

_____

_____

_____

_____

_____

_____

_____

Where were you located (city/town/country) when you had your first child?

_____

_____

_____

_____

SHARE SOME PARENTING PHOTOS HERE..

PARENTHOOD....

What has been the biggest challenge for you as a parent?

_____

_____

_____

_____

_____

_____

What are 3 key responsibilities you believe are important as a parent?

1 _____

_____

2 _____

_____

3 _____

_____

PARENTHOOD....

When did you first become a grandparent? Share some information about when you became a grandparent.

_____

_____

_____

Share a special grandparenting story.

_____

_____

_____

_____

_____

_____

_____

_____

_____

_____

_____

PARENTHOOD....

EXPAND ON ANY FURTHER PARENTING
MEMORIES YOU MAY LIKE TO SHARE

_____

_____

_____

_____

_____

_____

_____

_____

_____

_____

_____

_____

_____

_____

_____

_____

_____

MORE ABOUT ME!

ME TIME..

MORE ABOUT ME....

Not many people know this about me, so let me share it with you:

_____

_____

_____

_____

_____

_____

_____

The activity or hobby that I enjoy most to do now is.....

_____

_____

I have the unique ability to be able to....

_____

_____

_____

MORE ABOUT ME....

If I was able to go back to a special time in history, it would be...

_____

_____

_____

If I could pass on some of advice to others, it would be..

_____

_____

_____

There are special moments in life that you wish you could pause to enjoy for longer. Mine would be......

_____

_____

_____

_____

_____

MORE ABOUT ME....

I wish I had the opportunity to...

_____

_____

_____

The quote that resonates most with me is..

_____

_____

_____

_____

My favorite book of all time is:

_____

If there is one thing I would like to be remembered for
it would be:

_____

_____

_____

_____

MORE ABOUT ME....

In no particular order, these are some of my most proudest moments:

_____

_____

_____

_____

_____

_____

_____

_____

_____

_____

_____

_____

_____

_____

MORE ABOUT ME....

_____

_____

_____

_____

_____

_____

_____

_____

_____

_____

_____

_____

_____

_____

_____

_____

_____

MORE ABOUT ME....

My SUPER-POWER is the ability to.....

_____

_____

_____

_____

If there were 3 famous people that I could invite for dinner, they would be:

1 _____

2 _____

3 _____

MORE ABOUT ME....

From my teen years, these are the jobs that I've had:

_____

_____

_____

_____

_____

_____

_____

_____

_____

_____

_____

_____

_____

MORE ABOUT ME....

One of the jobs that stands out as my most enjoyable has been..

_____

_____

The most interesting place I have ever traveled to has been.... (include the year/date this occurred)

_____

_____

_____

If I was given a free return flight to anywhere in the world, I would visit...(include your 'Why')

_____

_____

_____

_____

_____

MORE ABOUT ME....

If I was granted 3 wishes, I would wish for....

_____

_____

_____

_____

_____

_____

If someone wrote a book about my life, the title of the book would be.....

SOME EXTRA SPACE FOR MORE INFORMATION OR PHOTOS HERE..

SOME EXTRA SPACE FOR MORE INFORMATION OR PHOTOS HERE..

FINAL NOTES

FINAL NOTES....

There have been many questions that I have answered in this book, but I would also like to share this with you...

Your time to write anything else you wish to share...

FINAL NOTES....

FINAL NOTES....

FINAL NOTES....

USE THE FOLLOWING PAGES FOR CERTIFICATES, AWARDS. PHOTO'S ETC..

THANK YOU FOR SHARING YOUR LIFE STORY

This book was created by

Romney Nelson

Book Review

JUST A REMINDER THAT IF YOU HAD THE OPPORTUNITY OF PROVIDING A REVIEW ON AMAZON IT WOULD BE GREATLY APPRECIATED. THANK YOU!

OTHER BOOKS
BY
The Life Graduate Publishing Group

THE LIFE GRADUATE
PUBLISHING GROUP

CPSIA information can be obtained
at www.ICGtesting.com
Printed in the USA
LVHW080103140222
711067LV00001B/5

9 781922 515896